I0414112

How to Pick Locks

by Tristan Trubble

Published in USA by:

Tristan Trubble
P.O BOX #9
Boynton Beach
FL 33425

© Copyright 2017

ISBN-13: 978-1548242145
ISBN-10: 1548242144

ALL RIGHTS RESERVED. No part of this publication may be reproduced or transmitted in any form whatsoever, electronic, or mechanical, including photocopying, recording, or by any informational storage or retrieval system without express written, dated and signed permission from the author.

Table of Contents

Introduction

You don't have to be a master criminal for the art of lock picking to come in handy. In the event of social collapse, there are no rules – the person with the right tools and skill set survives. In all actuality, it's not at all necessary for a burglar to master this skill, as easier ways than lock picking exist to break into your car or house. Any old rock or brick will do. But when it comes to clearing a locked door and covering your tracks in the process, this skill is not only handy, it's essential. To continue using the lock you've broken into, you'll want to keep it working soundly.

So, no, you don't have to be a criminal, and neither do you have to be an experienced locksmith to master the art. Instead, you can become what is commonly known as a "hacker." Much like computer hackers, those who pick locks recreationally do so as a hobby. Not only is it an extremely practical skill to have, once you get the hang of it, it's fun. Just keep your fun in check and don't push beyond hobby to breaking-and-entering, as to pick someone else's lock is a criminal offense, if you intend to steal anything within. However, as mentioned, if the worst of catastrophes should happen, breaking-and-entering will not be the issue – your survival will be.

In this book, you'll learn not only how to pick a lock, but the basic principles about locks and keys, how they work, and how easy it is to bust into nearly any lock. Knowing this may influence, in you, a whole new outlook on security.

Even with a lock or four on your door, you aren't completely safe. An experienced picker can break into anything using just a screwdriver and a paper clip or two. And, with the proper tools – like a lock picking kit with various pick tips and a torque wrench – they can break in even faster. Discovering how easy it is for even you to master lock picking may convince you that additional security measures should be taken when guarding your home and your valuables against invaders. A lock is not the be all, end all. You should always back up your backup.

This book will discuss not only techniques to picking a lock with a basic kit or with an electric pick gun, but also with your average everyday objects. A pick gun uses pieces of metal shaped like picks, which vibrate, pushing the pins up. This device might work instantly, or not at all, making it an unreliable strategy in emergency situations. A kit is the most useful, as it comes with a torque wrench and picks with different shaped heads which work in certain locks or improve technique; however, knowing how to break in using basic everyday tools, though a bit trickier, is something we'll cover as well.

Though not all locks are the same, the conceptualization of most locks is similar. The various shapes and sizes of locks does not mean that you'll have to learn a brand new strategy for each; you may just have to adjust a bit. Look at one simple lock, and you'll get the basic idea, as most work in the same way.

What most don't realize is that anyone can learn how to pick a lock. The common mechanical characteristics of a lock are what you, as a lock-picker, will be exploiting. So, in this book, we will identify these mechanical characteristics, and we will explain how to manipulate them. We will also look at exercises to practice your technique. If you want to become an advanced lock-picker, having the ability to unlock any lock in under thirty seconds isn't something you'll master on your first or second try. Practice makes perfect. Not only does practice make perfect, but having the right tools will significantly improve your technique. And you don't have to invest in a huge tool box either. We will discuss how to create your own lock picking tools out of everyday materials.

In the event of catastrophe or even in the event of everyday life, this skill may come to your aid when you're in desperate need of it. Will you be ready?

Chapter 1: Under Lock & Key

So how does a key open a lock? That's what we'll address in this chapter.

The vocabulary for the basic components of a lock varies between manufacturers and between locales, so refer to the diagram below if there's any confusion between manufacturer labels and this chapter's descriptions.

A Basic Cylindrical Lock (Pin Tumbler Lock)

We'll use a pin tumbler lock (a cylindrical lock) to discuss the device's inner workings, and the way a key opens a lock. Later on in the chapter, we'll talk about how picking can manipulate these inner workings.

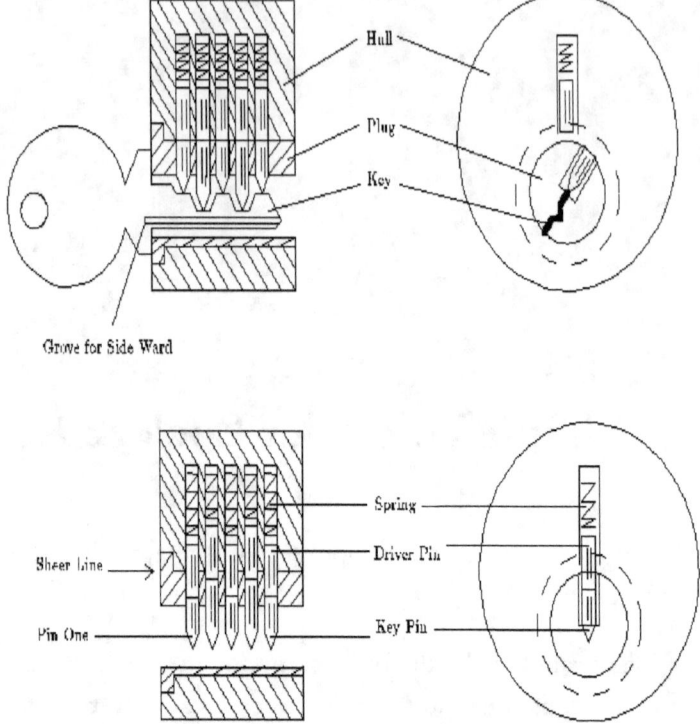

[not an approved image; reference for graphics department]

The cylindrical lock is often used by deadbolts and pin tumbler locks. As the cylinder (the plug) in a pin tumbler lock is turned by the key, the attached cam pulls the bolt in, opening the door. Likewise, if the cylinder or plug is turned the other way, the bolt is released by the cam, snapping a spring which locks the bolt into place. A deadbolt lock only has the cylinder to slide the bolt back and forth, not the spring, making a deadbolt more secure. A latch that's driven by a spring is easier to manipulate.

The first diagram shows the keyway of a plug. The keyway is like a puzzle for the key. The key is inserted into this keyway, which has protrusions called wards that interact with the key, restricting which key may open the lock. When the correct key is inserted, the cylindrical plug rotates, while the hull of the lock does not.

In a cylindrical lock, there is a series of paired pins, each pair of which sits in a shaft which is situated in the central plug down through to the plug's housing. The pairs are set by springs at the top of the shafts. If no key is inserted into the lock, each pair's bottom pin lies entirely inside the plug. The top pin protrudes halfway from the housing and halfway from the plug, so that the plug doesn't turn, but is secured to the housing.

The notches in a key press the pins to certain levels when the key is inserted in the lock. If you insert the wrong key, the top pins will be positioned partially in the housing and partially in the plug, so the lock's plug will not turn and the door will not open.

"Pin one" is the first pin the key touches, followed by the second, third, fourth and fifth (depending on how many pins the lock has). Each pin is lifted by the key until the space between the driver pin and the key pin closes at the shear line. Once all the pins have reached the shear line, the plug rotates, opening the lock. The pins' connection point must line up directly at this shear line, as it is the part of the lock where the housing and the cylinder connect. The pins must be on either side of the shear line – the lower pins entirely in the plug and the upper pins entirely in the house – or the lock will not open. If the wrong key is used, any one of the pins may not reach the shear line; instead they may protrude between the plug and the hull, preventing the rotation of the plug. With the right key, the pins are not holding the plug to the housing, so it can rotate, pulling the bolt out or pushing it in.

And so, a lock is effective to those who don't know how it works or how to manipulate it. But now that you know the basic components of a lock and key, learning how to pick it should be a no-brainer; all you must do is line those pins up along the shear line. However, it is important to note that the pins may vary on pin tumbler locks, making certain locks harder to pick than others. For instance, most pin tumblers have upper pins with mushroom heads. When you go to push the top pin up, the mushroom shape may cause the plug to shift before you've managed to clear the pin. This can be an issue when you're trying to get a feel for the inner workings of your lock, and especially when positioning the pins. Keep this in mind when practicing.

How to Pick a Pin Tumbler Lock

Being that in a pin tumbler lock, a key simply arranges the pins so that they line up along the shear line, this is what you'll be attempting to do with your torque wrench and pick – aligning each pair of pins into the correct position. You do this not all at once, but one pin at a time.

What is a torque wrench? A torque wrench is something which you can insert into the keyhole, turned slightly so that it offsets the plug a bit from the lock's housing. It's a simple tool that may come in all sizes, but is, in its simplest form, a very thin flathead screwdriver.

How about a pick? Picks must extend into the lock and press the pins up, so they are often thin scraps of metal, long and curving up at one end.

You can open the pin tumbler lock in four easy steps. Though the theory is simple, the practice may be a bit more difficult to master. Let's talk theory first.

Step 1: Insert Torque Wrench & Turn

First thing, turn your torque wrench in the key hole in the direction you would a key. As stated, this will offset the plug and the housing, producing in the pin shafts, a small ledge into which you can insert your pick and lift the pins.

Step 2: Insert Your Pick & Maneuver First Pin Pair

When inserting your pick, the aim is to raise each pair of pins to the point that the upper pin is shifted entirely into the housing, just as the right key would do. Apply slight pressure with your torque wrench and feel your way with your pick. Once you press the pin into the correct position, you'll either hear, or feel, the click of the pin moving into place on the shaft's ledge, which is what holds the upper pin in its housing. If it wasn't held securely in place, it would fall into the plug.

Step 3: Work Each Pin Pair into Place

Work your way through each pin pair, moving them into place along the shear line, with each of the top pins pressed into the housing, and each of the lower pins pressed into the plug.

Step 4: Open the Lock

Just as with the proper key, once all the pin pairs are aligned along the shear line, the plug will be allowed to rotate, opening the lock.

Technique

As you can see, the object is simple, but mastering the technique is the difficult part. You must learn, through practice, the exact amount of pressure to apply, and you must listen for the telltale click of the pins falling into place. While practicing, you must be able to visualize the working parts of the lock and its design. Furthermore, your sense of force must be honed, so that you can feel even the slightest movements of the pins and plug.

A second technique is called "raking." Locksmiths often start with this technique, which is faster and less precise than picking. The technique involves forcing a wide tip pick to the back of the plug. You then yank the pick out quickly with the aim to bounce the pins up as it's being pulled out. At the same time, using the torque wrench, you turn the plug so that the upper pins might fall on the ledge of the turning plug. If not all pins are caught, you can try raking the lock again or pick the rest individually.

Our first example is a simple cylindrical lock. We'll now look at different lock models to see how their mechanics and inner components vary, as you will have to adjust your own picking style and technique accordingly.

Chapter 2: Various Lock Models

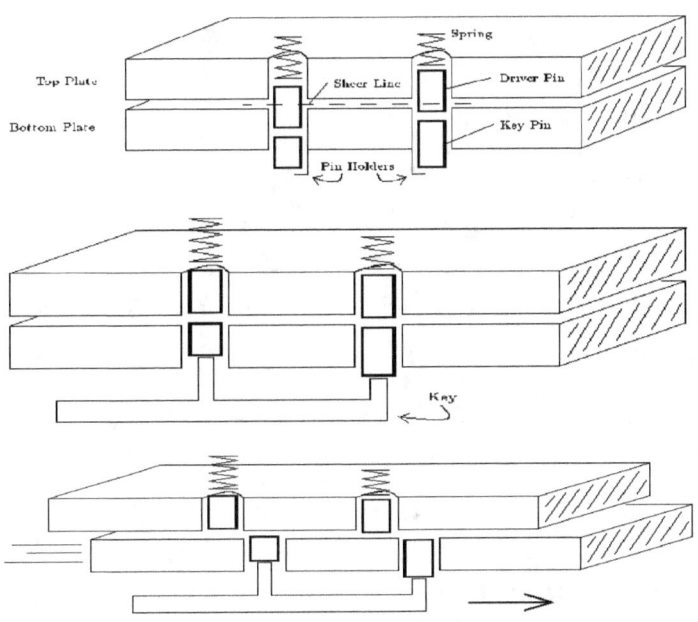

Flatland Model

Much like the cylindrical lock (or most locks, for that matter), the flatland model lock allows the proper key to open the lock through aligning metal pieces. In this case, two plates of metal are placed over each other and holes are drilled through both plates, creating a two hole lock in which two pins are placed. The gap between the plates doesn't align with the gap between the "key pin" (on the bottom) and the "driver pin" (on the top). The bottom plate has a protrusion beneath it to hold the pins in place, while the driver pin is pressed down by a spring over the top plate. These plates don't slide over each other, because the driver pins pass through both plates. As with any lock and key, the right key will raise the pin pairs, aligning them along the shear line.

Another important feature in a flatland lock is that the sliding allowance between the bottom and top plates means that various keys may open the lock. This also means the lock will be easier to pick, as you do not necessarily need to align the pins as precisely as in other locks, as shown in the third figure.

Wafer-Tumbler

The wafer-tumbler lock is another type of cylindrical lock, like the pin tumbler. In place of pins, however, it has wafer-shaped tumblers. Being that the keyhole is often wider in wafer-tumbler locks, the wafers are easier to pick than the pins of a pin tumbler. Wafer locks are found in most filing cabinets, lockers and cars, as well as in many padlock designs.

Depending on the design of your wafer-tumbler lock, the wafers may be single or in pairs, but they are always loaded by a spring, bound with the housing of the lock and extending out of the cylinder. With the proper key, the wafers are pulled down and retracted into the plug at just the right point. With the wrong key, the wafers will either be pulled down too far or not enough, so the plug will not be able to move.

If you run into a double-wafer lock, you'll have to use your torque wrench to apply pressure and work the wafers on both ends of the plug.

Tubular Locks

Often more expensive than wafer-tumbler and pin tumbler locks, when it comes to security, you get more bang for your buck with a tubular lock, as it's more complex and difficult to pick. The cylinder plug is lined not with a single row of pins, but along the plug's entire circumference. The above mentioned lock picking technique does not often work on a tubular lock.

Pin Column Lock

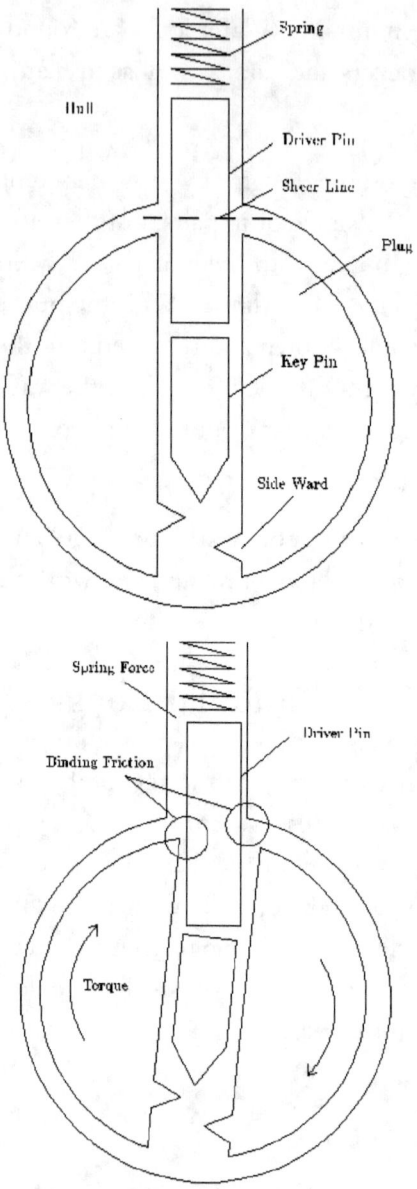

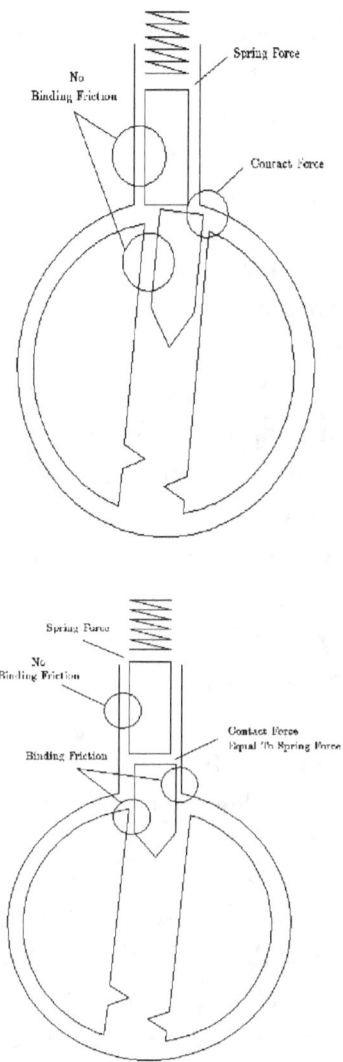

The previously mentioned models hold more than one pin, but a pin column lock holds a single pin, which may demonstrate the correlation between the application of torque and the force required to lift the pin. The "feel" of picking depends on this relationship. As a lock-picker, knowing how a pin is manipulated by both the pressure of your pick in combination with the torque from your wrench is key...no pun intended.

The pin's displacement from its original position is directly related to the pressure required to move it. In a pin-column model, there are three forces acting upon the driver pin: the spring force from above the pin, the side friction surrounding the pin, and the force from the key pin below. When the pins are pressed into the hull, the spring force grows. The pins will move only if you apply the right amount of pressure to combat the spring force. When you apply torque, friction is creating pressure between the driver pin, the plug and the hole, making the pins more difficult to move; however, you need to apply pressure to counter the friction and the spring for the pins to align. Only the correct amount will do for the bottom of the driver pin to align with the shear line, allowing the plug to rotate.

In any other lock type, a second pin will then bind the lock. Though the friction of the first pin is no longer an issue, the spring force is still there, as is the new force which comes from the key pin rubbing against the hull. This means, to move the next pin, you will need to increase the pressure. But a pin column lock has a single pin, so once you've applied enough pressure to align the pin along the shear line, you've jimmied the lock and allowed the plug to move.

Chapter 3: Set-Up & Practice

Before we get into the further details of lock characteristics, let's get some practical experience under your belt. You'll first need to set up your work station. Gathering the materials you'll need will help you to visualize the process and the mechanics of various lock types.

Assemble Your Tools

Torque Wrench

You don't necessarily need a lock pick set; instead, you can replace the requisite torque wrench with an Allen wrench, a paper clip or a screwdriver. With the Allen wrench, you can use a grinder or a file to grind the wrench down to size – it must be able to enter the key-way. The width should be ground down to the point that it can enter; no more, no less. You can also use a sturdy paper clip. You'll have to straighten it out and bend a loop in one end large enough to slide into the key-way. The remainder of the wire should be bent about 90 degrees at the loop's end. A small screwdriver can be used as well, but make sure it's big enough to touch the wards, as you'll want to be able to turn it with enough pressure.

Pick

To pick your first pin, you can use any number of tools, but when you advance to the second, you'll need to upgrade your pick. But let's not get ahead of ourselves. An Allen wrench, a paper clip, a screw driver, a safety pin, a straight pin, or a staple can be used as a pick. If you're using an Allen wrench or screw driver, you should choose the smallest one available. A paper clip or staple will need to be sturdy enough to handle the springs' force and should be straightened out flat. A safety pin or straight pin should have the point filed off so you don't prick yourself.

Purchase a Lock

Purchase a lock to practice on, one which will help you identify the lock's components. You're likely to damage the lock in the process of exploring it, so don't spend too much money on it, and don't use one if you want it to work again. We suggest that you start with a deadbolt five pin tumbler (most deadbolts are this lock type), which you can purchase at any department store. Don't go too cheap, as cheap locks are often difficult to operate, even with a key. A generic or Kwikset deadbolt lock will be easier to disassemble.

Remove All Pins Except One

Remember, you're a newbie, so don't get in over your head. Picking a five-pin tumbler is something you'll master down the line, but first off, you'll start by picking one pin. In this way, you'll develop a sense of picking successfully, as it's difficult at first to get the feel for it. Don't destroy your lock when removing the pins. Leave the pin closest to the lock's front in so that you'll be able to see the process as you work.

Pick Your First Pin

Take what you've learned so far from this manual and put it into practice. You might try working with the lock upside down, as it's sometimes easier. Press your torque wrench a bit into the lock and insert your pick, while slowly lowering the first pin. You'll know when you've nailed the shear line, as the plug will turn. And, there you have it. You can practice repeatedly by returning the plug to its locked position and picking it again.

Attempt Multiple Pins

You've got the feel of it now, so you can add another pin into the mix, behind the first pin. Again, do not get ahead of yourself; practice bit by bit to become proficient. It may take you a few days to master the five-pin pick, and you'll need an advanced set of tools to do so. You're likely to be able to pick three pins with the household materials mentioned, but if you want to advance past that, then you should order a pick set while practicing for the feel of it.

Chapter 4: Scrubbing

The different models we've discussed reveal the defects in locks, which allow your average locksmith or lock-pick enthusiast to manipulate them. By lifting the pins, one by one, you need neither key nor high tech tools to unlock your normal everyday lock. All you need is a little patience and practice.

Though practicing at home has no time constraints, when you're in a bind, time is of the essence. We'll talk a little in this chapter about how to speed up the process of picking through a technique called scrubbing.

Scrubbing is when the correct amount of pressure is applied as you run the pick over all the pins, enough to counter the friction and spring forces, but slightly less than the collision force of the key pin colliding with the hull. The technique usually requires a lock-picker who is practiced enough to have a feel for the proper torque and pick force. By expertly applying these measures, when your pick crosses over a pin, the pin will lift and hit the hull but not enter it, causing the plug to rotate which will catch the driver pin on the plug's edge, just above the shear line. In this way, with one swipe of the pick across the pins, the lock will open. Of course, this only applies to those who have become an expert hand at scrubbing. Even then, a lot of the time only one or two pins will set in the first scrub and several additional scrubs may be necessary, with readjustments to the amount of torque you're applying to the plug.

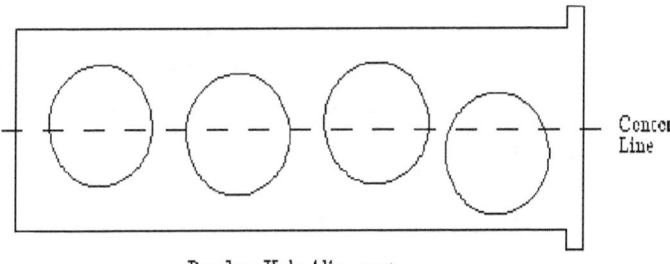

Center
Line

Ideal Hole Alignment

Center
Line

Hole Axis Skewed From Center Line

Center
Line

Random Hole Alignment

This method is quick, because instead of focusing on individual pins, you're only required to nail down the proper pressure and torque. If a lock does not open through this method, then you will have to take it pin by pin. You will notice that a lock's pins set in a certain order, which is often affected by a misalignment between the axis of the drilled holes and those of the plug's center axis. This defect means that the pins will set from front to back if turned one way and the opposite if turned the other way, depending on the skew of the pin holes and the plug's center line.

Below are step-by-step instructions on this faster and more efficient technique.

Step 1: Test Your Lock

Insert the torque wrench and pick. Before you apply torque, sense the strength of the lock's springs by pulling the pick out.

Step 2: Apply Some Torque

Employ a light amount of torque and insert the pick being careful not to touch the pins. Yank the pick out swiftly while applying enough pressure to combat the spring force, but not too much.

Step 3: Increase Torque

With each scrub, apply more and more torque until the pins start to set in place. The driver pins should catch on the plug.

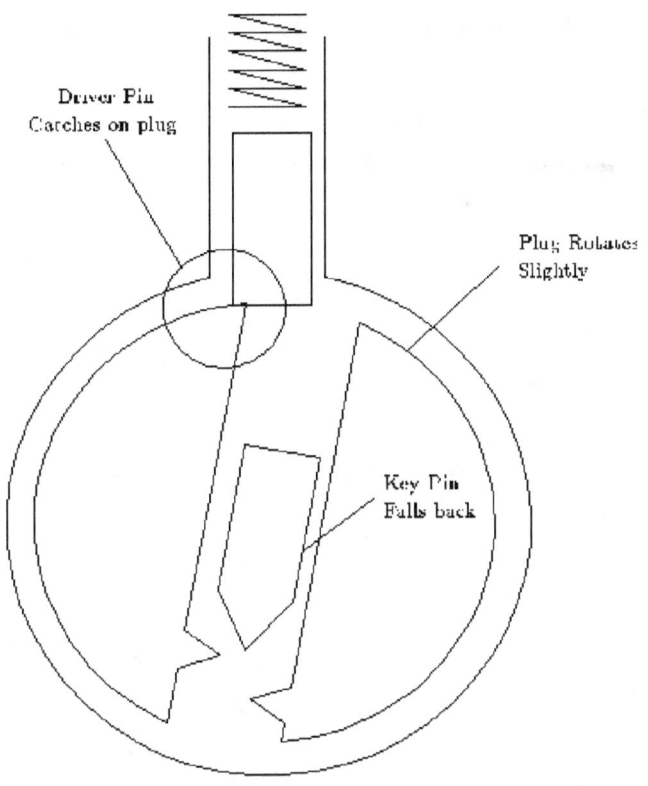

Driver Pin
Catches on plug

Plug Rotates
Slightly

Key Pin
Falls back

Step 4: Scrub

Maintain your torque and scrub across the pins that have
yet to set. If they do not set, lighten the torque a bit.

Step 5: Apply More Torque & Pressure

When most of the pins have set, apply more torque again and more pressure on the pins. Doing so should set those pins which have beveled edges and are set lower.

Chapter 5: Exercises

Now that you've tried picking and scrubbing, it's time to hone your skills. As practice is key to lock picking, the following series of exercises will help you master your technique. Instead of focusing on the result – opening the lock – focus on developing your skills when working through these exercises. Doing so will allow you to better your knowledge and feel for the lock without becoming frustrated and throwing in the towel. Practice in short bursts of thirty minutes or so; otherwise your fingers and mind will be stiff, tense, and not at all conducive to learning the art of lock picking.

Exercise 1: Getting a Feel for Torque

A common mistake for beginner pickers is to use excessive and consistent amounts of torque, without adjusting the level. A range of torque is required to open a lock, and it is necessary to coordinate the amount of torque with the amount of pressure of the pick and with the other forces inherently influential within the lock.

You will need to apply the minimum amount of torque to combat the friction of the plug's rotation in the hull. Insert your torque wrench into the plug, and note the amount of torque necessary to rotate the plug before the pins bind. Some locks may require more torque than others, such as those with water damage due to rain or snow. When it comes to padlocks, the minimum torque required should account for the spring's force, which connects the shackle bolt and the plug.

The high end of your torque pressure can be found by using the pick's flat side to press all the pins down, and once the pick is removed, attempting to employ a significant amount of torque to force those pins to remain down. This should result in the key pins being pressed deep into the hull, where the torque holds them; thus, the torque and pressure is too much. Testing this max torque will help you identify the accurate level of torque to apply – somewhere between the minimum amount first tested in rotating the plug and the maximum amount tested here.

Using the scrubbing technique will also help you assess the range of torque required. You can apply more and more torque gradually while using your pick to scrub the pins until some of the pins set. Certain pins will become increasingly more difficult to press down, and finally, will lose their springiness altogether. Once you arrive at that point, maintain your level of torque, and scrub the pins several more times with the pick until they set.

Getting a feel for torque is essential to lock picking, so practice until you are comfortable with its application.

Exercise 2: Getting a Feel for Pick Pressure

As with torque, it's necessary to apply a range of pressure to your pick. In the beginning, only apply your pick pressure when pulling the pick from the lock and, when you've got that down, you can attempt to apply pressure on insertion as well.

With your pick and torque wrench in the lock, press the first pin of a lock down using your pick's flat side, without applying any torque. This pressure should just combat the spring force, allowing you to feel out the minimum amount of pick pressure to apply. As you press the pin, the spring force will increase, so test out the levels of pressure required to press all the pins down as you draw the pick from the lock. As the pick is withdrawn, the pins will spring back, producing a sound. Feel out each pin with your pick – they will spring as the pick presses them down, and they will pop as the pick brushes past them. This is the minimum pressure required of your pick.

To test the maximum pressure, press all the lock pins at a single time with the flat side of your pick. A single pin may require an application of this amount of pressure, depending on the springs' stiffness. New locks may possess stiffer springs, meaning an increase in pick pressure is essential.

Exercise 3: Applying Fixed Pick Pressure

Learning how to bounce the pick will help you master the application of fixed pick pressure as it moves in the lock. Each pin may have varied resistance, so the pressure you apply to them with your pick will have to bounce according to this resistance. Never focus on the handle movement of a pick, but only on a pick's tip, as this is the crucial point of picking.

The way in which you hold your pick significantly affects the ease by which pressure is applied. Hold your pick so that the pressure applied extends from your wrist or fingers, not your shoulder or elbows. When you scrub a lock, take note of those finger joints that are used and those that are fixed. The used joints will need to be strong and agile enough to apply the pressure.

You might try holding your pick with three fingers – one to lever the pick, allowing the pressure to be applied, and two to enable a pivot point for the pick. Or, you can simply hold your pick like a pencil, with the pressure being applied by your wrist and the movement being provided by your elbow and shoulder. The wrist should not be used for both movement and pressure application.

Again, you can use the scrubbing technique to get the feel for the bouncing of the pick in the keyway. Make sure your lock is open so that the pins don't press down. In this way, the pick will scrub across the pins' varied heights, rattling as the pick brushes them. This rattle sound and feel is what you will hear when a pin is set accurately. Though a pin may look as though it is set, without the rattle, the pin is set falsely, and you will need to fix this either by releasing torque so that they return to their original position or pressing them down more.

Exercise 4: Determining Which Pins are Set

The ability to determine which pins are set is the most important factor of picking locks. When practicing, take note on the identification of set pins. You will know which, as the pin will have a slight give; you will be able to press it down slightly with little pressure, after which it won't move any further. Once you remove the little pressure applied, the pin will spring back slightly. You will also be able to determine when a pin is set by flicking them with your pick and hearing their rattle. This rattling sound will help you identify set pins from unset or falsely set ones.

When you are attempting to determine at which part of the lock the pins are set – the front or the back – you can run your pick over the pins to feel and listen for these identifying factors. Repeat the process with the plug turned in the opposite direction. When the back pins set with the plug turned one direction, the front pins will set with the plug turned opposite; and vice versa.

If you are unsure about how many pins are set, remove the torque and note how many clicks sound. These clicks are the pins returning to their original positions. There will be different sounds when multiple pins snap back and when a single pin does. False set pins will also snap back. Being able to recognize the number of snaps or clicks will allow you to determine how many pins you still need to set.

You can repeat this exercise applying various amounts of pressure and torque. The larger the amount of torque applied, the more pressure required to set the pins. With a high amount of pressure, the pins will be lodged in the hull and unmovable.

Exercise 5: Visualization

In addition to working through these exercises, visualizing the process of what you're doing is key to understanding the inner workings of the lock. To assist in the visualization, once you've successfully opened a lock, you should recount in your mind both the physicality of the process and the connections you made in your assessment of the pins setting. Instead of simply being satisfied with the result, think about what you did and what happened within the lock so that you can improve upon your next attempt.

Your visualization skills will need to be refined to advance to master lock picking, so consider practicing these skills by using a simple lock, one easy enough to pick. Recall the visual and sensational process of properly picking the lock and go over it again, step-by-step in your mind, noting both the pressure and torque application, the pick's resistance, and the feel of the pins setting. Once you have your visualization vivid in your mind, try picking the lock again with this thought process directing your actions. Doing so will allow you to command your pressure and your muscles, and will enable you to assess your senses, both hearing and touch. Visualization of both the process and the lock's working parts will hone your picking process by providing you a basis by which to determine what's going on within the lock and the steps required to successfully open it.

Chapter 6: Master Lock Picking

Once you're proficient in the basics of lock picking, advancing to master lock picking means that you must craft your mechanics, analytical thinking and visualization. These are the traits that differentiate between someone who can pick at their own pace from someone who can pick with the speed and agility an emergency requires.

Mechanics

The mechanics of picking, and especially of scrubbing, are not as easy as one may think. The mechanical skills and dexterity acquired in youth require one to hold their hands in a fixed position separate from force. However, being that you must apply a fixed pressure on the pins when you remove the pick from the lock, lock picking requires the application of a fixed force free from your hands' positioning. You must be able to allow the pick to bounce in the keyway in direct response to each pin's resistance.

To hone your mechanical skills, assess the feel and sound of your manipulations between your pick and the pins. With practice, your fingers will gain the knowledge that's essential to move from basic to advanced lock picking.

Analytical Thinking

Locks vary, as do the difficulties in picking them. However, being able to identify and exploit the characteristics of certain styles or brands of lock will make the rest of the process much quicker. This is where analytical thinking comes in. To become a better picker, you'll need to be able to determine a lock's characteristics by analyzing the feedback that's sent to your fingers during your manipulation of the lock. The more familiar you become with the characteristics of various locks, the easier it will be to analyze your picking and readjust your approach.

Think of your tools as both analytical and practical. As you run your pick over the pins, it is gathering the information about the lock. This analysis can then be used to adjust the torque from the torque wrench, which will set the pins at the shear line and open the lock. For instance, if you should find through your analysis that the middle pins are set in place, but the end pins have yet to set, when you move the pick over the middle pins, you should increase the torque so that the set pins are not unset in the process. You can also reduce the torque if you feel that a certain pin isn't raising enough when the pick crosses over it. The variation of torque is paramount to setting all pins in place, and the process of pinpointing the correct amount is as much an analytical one as a physical one, requiring precise coordination and even more precise analysis.

Visualization

As mentioned in the section on basic lock picking, visualization will not only help you open the lock in the moment; it will also help you to review and analyze your process. Through sensual information – those of your hands, eyes and ears –, you can make connections in your mind about the lock's inner workings and your manipulations. Your ears and hands will tell you when a pin is set, your eyes will help you better coordinate your efforts, especially in the beginning. All senses, combined, will aid your visualization, which will then provide in you a concentration that is both relaxed and focused, helping you to make the correct moves to open the lock.

Chapter 7: Lock Characteristics

To develop your advanced skills, you will need to know the various characteristics of different locks. This range of characteristics is what will determine your approach to each lock. Those locks that cannot be scrubbed often have one or more of the characteristics listed below. Our advice will help you to both identify the lock's features and apply the right methods to combat the lock's characteristics.

The Direction of the Plug's Rotation

When you pick a lock, you should first find which way the plug rotates, otherwise you'll have spent time and effort with no result. The bolt mechanism is what determines the direction the plug should rotate. You can determine the correct rotation by turning the plug and assessing whether it rotates freely until it stops. This is the wrong way. When you turn the plug the right way, you will sense resistance, as the bolt spring and plug cam interact.

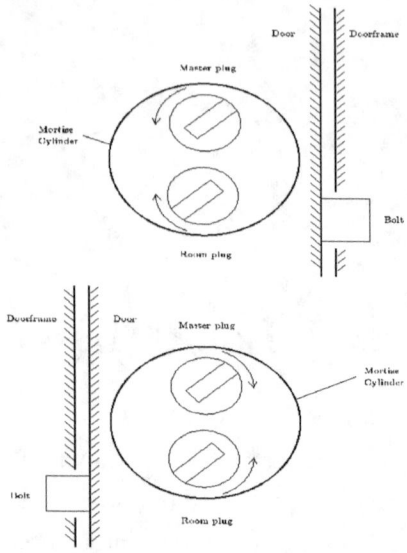

Certain locks can be picked no matter which way you turn the plug. Some padlocks (such as those by the Master brand), for instance, work either way, so choose whichever is easier to work with your torque wrench. Yale padlocks, on the other hand, only open with a clockwise rotation. Locks that are built into a doorknob or are built into filing cabinets or desks often require a clockwise rotation, while single plug cylinder locks usually open when the keyway's bottom (the key's flat edge) is rotated away from the doorframe.

If you are faced with a new brand or model of lock, rotate the plug in either direction and analyze the result. A full solid stop will result when the plug is turned in the wrong direction, while the right direction will result in a springy stop, one where you can feel the pins stopping the turn when you use torque.

The Extent of the Plug's Rotation

Now that you know which direction you need to turn your plug, to what extent should you turn it? A complete turn is often required of deadbolt locks, while a filing cabinet or desk lock often requires only a 90-degree turn (a quarter) or less, as do locks built into the doorknob. A lock that's independent of the doorknob often requires a half-turn to open it.

Scrubbing Doesn't Set Pins

When scrubbing does not set the pins of the lock, even with torque variation, it is often the case that a pin has falsely set, which inhibits the other pins from setting. For instance, in a lock with pins that set from front to back, if the first pin false sets either low or high, the remaining pins cannot set, because the plug cannot turn enough to allow them to bind. If this circumstance arises, start the process over again and focus on the front pins, applying varied amounts of torque and pressure until you feel the pin set along the shear line and the slight rotation of the plug. A stiff torque wrench will give you a better feel for the pin setting.

Springs & Gravity

Locks sometimes have the springs at the bottom and others have them at the top. Those with the springs at the bottom are sometimes easier to manipulate, as once you've set the key pins, gravity holds them down, making it simpler to differentiate between set pins and unset ones. This arrangement also allows for easier testing of set pins. Gravity also comes into play when the springs are at the top; only this time gravity forces the key pins down once the driver pin is at the shear line, and you must lift the key pin to see that they're set. Either way, you can hear the rattle of a set pin by drawing your pick across them. They rattle because the driver pin is no longer pressing them down.

Elasticity

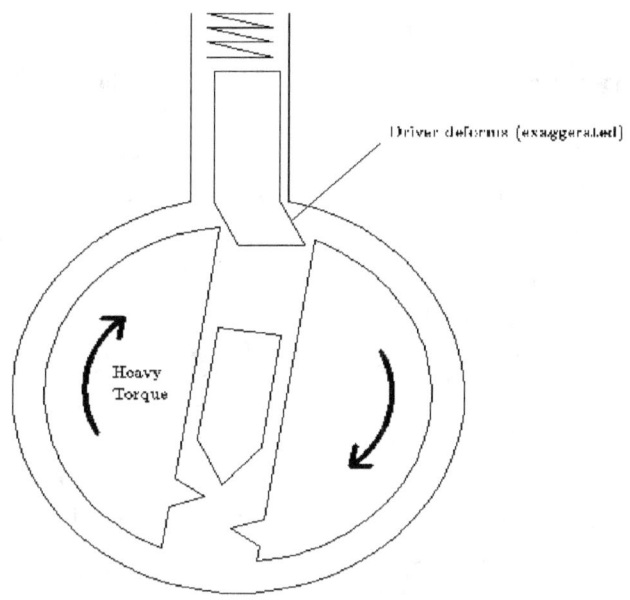

Driver pin is false set by elasticity

Because lock picking involves measures in the thousandths of an inch, metals have elasticity like springs, in that only minute amounts of force are required to direct the metal, which will spring back to its initial position once that force is no longer influencing it. If you want multiple pins to set at a single time, you can use this elasticity to your advantage. For instance, if you're picking a lock whose pins set from front to back, you'll find that the process is slow, as one pin will set at a time if you apply pressure only when drawing the pick from the lock. The foremost pin will be set, while many other passes may set the rest of the pins. However, if your plug's holes are only slightly off axis of the plug's center, applying a little extra torque will twist the plug, causing the front pin columns to bend just enough for the back of the plug to turn enough so that the back pins set. So that extra bit of torque can allow a single scrub of the pick to set multiple pins, which means your lock will open quicker. Too much torque and too little torque will prevent multiple pins from setting.

Loose Plug

There is a hole drilled into the hull which holds the plug; the plug is wider in the front with a cam on the back that is larger than the hole. Sometimes the cam of the lock is not installed properly, so the plug moves slightly in the lock. This means that the plug may move when you insert the pick and when you remove it, which means that the driver pins will unset. In these loose plugs, rather than being set on the sides of the holes, the driver pins often set on the back of the plug holes. To avert this issue, either hold the plug using your finger or torque wrench so that it doesn't move or only apply pressure upon insertion of the pick or upon its removal.

Pin Diameter

In certain cases, a pin pair will have differing diameters, hindering the pins' movement. The key pin may have a larger diameter, or vice versa. The issue here is that the key pin may stick in the hull when another pin sets, as the plug may rotate just enough to bind the thinner key pin when the pick is pressing down on the set pin. Navigating this issue is an exercise for the patient and advanced lock-picker.

Rounded Pins & Beveled Holes

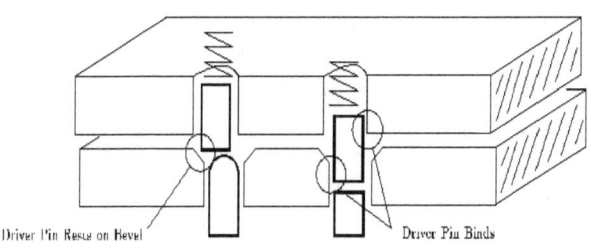

Driver Pin Rests on Bevel   Driver Pin Binds

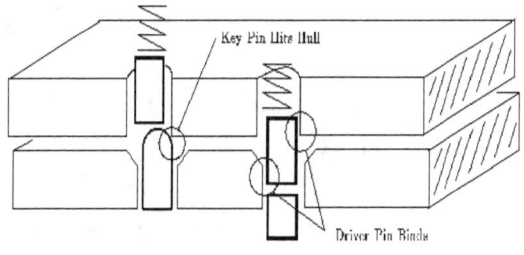

Key Pin Hits Hull

Driver Pin Binds

The edges of the plug holes may be beveled in some products, while the ends of the key pins may be rounded, to decrease the wear and tear on the lock. The lock may have either of these features if set pins provide a lot of give, being that there is a larger gap between the driver pin and the plug hole, and the key pin and the hull. This means that the spring's force will be the only resistance on the key pin as it moves between the two, requiring less force.

However, more scrubbing is required with a beveled plug hole, as instead of setting on the top of the plug, the driver pins set on the bevel, which means the plug won't be able to turn. To move the driver pin off the bevel, you must scrub the key pin again.

When all pins seem to be set in a lock with beveled plug holes, and yet the lock hasn't unlocked, scrub across the pins again while reducing torque, so that the drivers can be pushed off the bevels. Pins may unset when torque is reduced, so increase the pressure of your pick and the torque and try again.

Mushroom Driver Pins

Lock manufacturers change the shape of the driver pin to make it more difficult to pick. You may come across spool, serrated and mushroom shapes, which false set low. Though you may not be able to vibration pick these types of pins, you will still be able to scrub the pins or pick them one at a time. Recognizing the modified pins is the key to picking these types of locks, so you should practice determining if your lock has modified drivers. A normal driver will have a springy give, while a mushroom driver will not.

You know that the driver pins have a varied shape if you can only turn the plug a little and no pins can be pressed up.

It won't budge, as the lip of the driver is stuck on the shear line. By applying a little torque, push up on each pin; those with mushroom drivers will lock the plug's position. When you press the key pin up, the key pin's flat top is pressing against the mushroom driver's curved bottom, which straightens the driver and unwinds the plug. By noting which of the pin columns cause this unwinding, you can pinpoint which have mushroom drivers and push these pins to the shear line. If, in the process, other pins unset, you can repick them much easier than the mushroom drivers.

When you have modified drivers, you should use a heavy pick pressure and a light torque. You'd rather push the key pins farther into the hull than not far enough. A second way to approach modified drivers is to press the pins all the way up with your pick's flat side, applying heavier torque to keep them in place. Then slowly decrease the level of torque to reduce the binding friction and vibrate the key pins by scrubbing. The key pins will be forced slowly down to the shear line through the spring force and vibration.

Master Keys

An extra pin, or a "spacer," is required in some locks to accommodate a master key. A change key opens a single lock, while a master key opens numerous locks. The spacer is included so that both a change key and a master key can be allowed to open the lock. With a spacer, the pin column has two gaps which may line up with the shear line. In most cases, the master key draws the bottom of the spacer to the shear line, while the change key draws the top of it to the shear line. In this way, a change key cannot be filed down to alter it into an illegal master key. The plug rotates freely whether a change or master key is used.

For the most part, you can pick these locks easier, as a spacer increases the options to set a pin and makes it more probable that a picker can set all the pins at nearly the same height to open the lock. Often only a couple pin pairs will have spacers, which you can sniff out by listening or feeling for two clicks when you press the pin down. Most often, the driver pin is smaller than the spacer, which you'll notice through increased friction when the spacer crosses the shear line. This also allows the driver pin to catch on the plug easier. A hard click will be felt if you press the spacer past the shear line into the hull.

Sometimes the driver and key pins will be larger in diameter than the spacer, which you'll notice through feel, as the spacer won't bind when crossing the shear line. In this case, the spacer can jam on the shear line if heavy torque is applied and the plug holes are beveled. The spacer may even fall into the keyway when the plug is turned halfway. See section 9.11 for the solution to this problem.

Spacer or Driver is in the Keyway

When you rotate the plug halfway, a driver pin or spacer can enter the keyway. This can be prevented, however, simply by putting your pick's flat side in the bottom of the keyway before you rotate the plug by 180 degrees. Relieve the shear force that's acting on the driver or spacer with your torque wrench, and use your pick's flat side to press the spacer into the hull. If the spacer or driver is still in the keyway, scrub the drivers with your pick's pointed end. You may need to remove the spacer with a hooked paper clip or spring steel if it falls entirely into the keyway.

Vibration Picking

By making a gap between the driver and key pins, you can use vibration picking to flick all the pins' tips, much like when a queue ball drives another ball off in pool; if hit squarely, the ball is driven at the same speed as the queue ball was traveling, while the queue ball stops dead in its tracks. If you vibration pick the pins, each key pin will knock into their corresponding driver pins, springing them up into the hull. By applying slight torque at the same time, the driver pins will align above the shear line, and the plug will turn.

Chapter 8: Tools

As you advance to a master level of lock picking, so must your tools. Below is a list of various lock picking tools and what they can do for you.

Torque wrenches

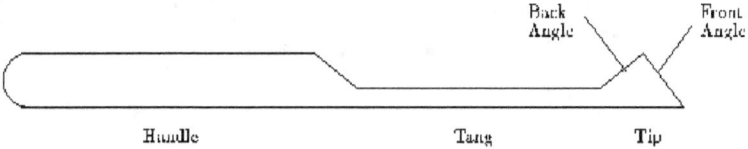

The handle of a torque wrench can run anywhere from 2 to 4 inches, while the head is often between ½ to ¾ of an inch long. The longer the handle, the more precisely you can control the torque; however, too long, and your handle may hit the doorframe. The head is rather short, but must be able to extend past protrusions (a grip-proof collar, for example) to insert into the plug. How well the width of the torque wrench's head will fit into the lock depends on the lock. Some, like file cabinet or desk locks, require a narrow head. An 80-degree bend separates the handle and the head, while some have a handle twist of 90 degrees, which makes the handle like a spring, controlling the torque easier. With the handle twist, however, you don't feel as much feedback in the plug's rotation.

You can make your own torque wrench with 8-penny nail with a diameter of .1   inch. With a propane torch or a gas stove, fire your wrench's point until it's red, take it slowly from the fire, and allow it to cool and soften. Then grind the metal into a thin screwdriver shaped blade, bending it at 80 degrees. Do not bend it to a right angle, as the wrench's head should extend at least a half inch into the plug, and a plate sometimes recesses a lock face, hindering this reach. Next, you should fire your wrench to orange and then dip it in ice water to harden or temper your wrench. This torque wrench will be super strong and can be used for years to come.

Pick Shapes

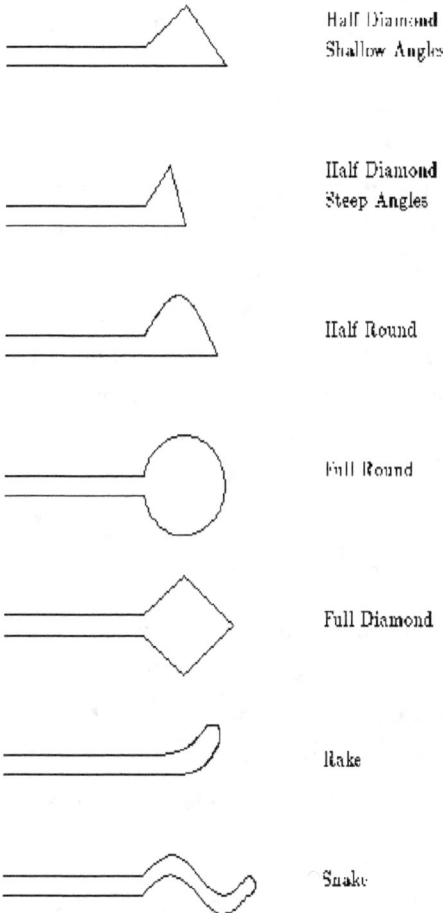

Half Diamond
Shallow Angles

Half Diamond
Steep Angles

Half Round

Full Round

Full Diamond

Rake

Snake

There are many different sizes and shapes of picks to choose from, although the handle and tang are the same. The tang should be thin, so that it doesn't bump the pins, but not too thin, or it will be like a spring, and you won't be able to obtain an accurate feel of the pick against the pins. The handle should be comfortable and convenient to work with.

The tip of the pick's shape will determine how you feel the pins and the ease by which the pick crosses the pins. A tip's design will guide you to the pick that's right for you and for the lock you're opening. For example, locks that have pins on both sides of the keyway are best opened using a full-round or full diamond tip, while a disk tumbler lock is best opened by a half-round tip. When you need to pick pins one at a time or raked over the pins, the rake tip is best. In the latter use, only apply pressure when you withdraw the pick. The rake tip is also great if you don't want to leave traces of your picking, because the rake tip aligns well on the pin and so doesn't scratch the pins or spread metal dust, especially when picking one-by-one. You can either use a dented or flat rake tip.

If you don't care about leaving traces, then you'll want to scrub, which is great for opening household locks with five pins. A snake tip can also be used for picking; it'll set multiple pins at one time, because when you lower or raise the tip, the pick acts like a key segment when you use strong torque.

Half diamond picks tips, for example can be steep or shallow. The steep angles give you a better feeling for the pins, while shallow angles provide easier insertion and removal, allowing you to apply pressure either way. If there are small variations in a lock's key pins, the shallow angled tip will pick the lock easily; however, if a lock has large variations – like a deep dip between two shallow dips – the middle pin may not be effectively pushed down by a shallow-angled tip, making the steep-angled pick your best bet. A steep-angled tip has its disadvantages too; it can be more difficult to manipulate in the lock.

If you're in need of a makeshift pick, try using a bicycle spoke by simply bending it to the shape you require, and file one end flat. The horizontal of the pick should be flexible, while the vertical should be strong. You can bend an inch-long triangle into a handle.

Conclusion

As you read this book, you've probably concluded that the basics of lock picking are quite simple. It doesn't take a mastermind to pick a lock. Anyone with half a brain, a steady hand, and a bit of tenacity can learn how to break into basic locks. However, the art of advanced lock picking – that of speed, agility, and an acute sense of touch – does require practice and some level of concentration. Thus, time and patience are necessary to learning the trade.

When the world comes crashing down, there's no greater tool to add to your toolbelt than being able to open any lock you come across. But the world doesn't necessarily have to come CRASHING down for the skill to be incredibly useful. In everyday life, lock picking can be a lifesaver in any emergency where the thing that stands between you and your property or you and freedom is a lock.

In this book, we've talked about the lock and key, how they work, and how to manipulate them. We've delivered the step-by-step processes of picking a lock pin by pin and scrubbing a lock's pins all at once. We've identified and compared different types of locks, and we've examined their mechanical parts. We've sorted out the very best lock picking tools and even explained how you might make your own pick and torque wrench. And, finally, we've also discussed the various characteristics of a lock and what you, as a lock picker, can do to exploit these characteristics, speeding your process along. Though new lock models are always being made, and you may come across a model that wasn't covered in this book, you'll still be able to use the basic knowledge you've learned to navigate new territory.

Anyone can learn how to pick a lock, but it's practicing technique and honing your advanced lock picking skills – mechanics, visualization and analytical thinking – that will set you apart from your average picker. There's no point in learning a new skill, if you let it rust. So always practice and don't lose your "feel" for lock picking so that you might face the worst case scenario head-on when it comes rushing into meet you.

ALL RIGHTS RESERVED. No part of this publication may be reproduced or transmitted in any form whatsoever, electronic, or mechanical, including photocopying, recording, or by any informational storage or retrieval system without express written, dated and signed permission from the author.

DISCLAIMER AND/OR LEGAL NOTICES: Every effort has been made to accurately represent this book and it's potential. Results vary with every individual, and your results may or may not be different from those depicted. No promises, guarantees or warranties, whether stated or implied, have been made that you will produce any specific result from this book. Your efforts are individual and unique, and may vary from those shown. Your success depends on your efforts, background and motivation.

The material in this publication is provided for educational and informational purposes only and is not intended as medical advice. The information contained in this book should not be used to diagnose or treat any illness, metabolic disorder, disease or health problem. Always consult your physician or health care provider before beginning any nutrition or exercise program. Use of the programs, advice, and information contained in this book is at the sole choice and risk of the reader.

www.ingramcontent.com/pod-product-compliance
Lightning Source LLC
Chambersburg PA
CBHW071116280526
45787CB00003B/1071